DISCOVERING CANADA

The Rebels

ROBERT LIVESEY & A.G. SMITH

Stoddart Kids

TORONTO • NEW YORK

*We acknowledge for their financial support of our publishing program the
Government of Canada through the Book Publishing Industry Development
Program (BPIDP), the Canada Council, and the Ontario Arts Council.*

Published in Canada in 2000 by
Stoddart Kids,
a division of Stoddart Publishing Co. Limited
895 Don Mills Rd., 4th Floor
North York, Ontario M3C 1W3
Tel (416) 445-3333 Fax (416) 445-5967
E-mail cservice@genpub.com

Distributed in Canada by
General Distribution Services
325 Humber College Blvd.
Toronto, Ontario M9W 7C3
Tel (416) 213-1919 Fax (416) 213-1917
E-mail cservice@genpub.com

Published in the United States in 2000 by
Stoddart Kids,
a division of Stoddart Publishing Co. Limited
180 Varick Street, 9th Floor
New York, New York 10014
Toll free 1-800-805-1083
E-mail gdsinc@genpub.com

Distributed in the United States by
General Distribution Services, PMB 128
4500 Witmer Industrial Estates
Niagara Falls, New York 14305-1386
Toll free 1-800-805-1083
E-mail gdsinc@genpub.com

04 03 02 01 00 1 2 3 4 5

Canadian Cataloguing in Publication Data

Livesey, Robert, 1940 –
The rebels

(Discovering Canada)
Includes index.
ISBN 0-7737-6170-5

1. Canada – Biography – Juvenile literature. 2. Canada – History – Juvenile literature.
I. Smith, A.G. (Albert Gray,) 1945 –   . II. Title. III. Series: Livesey, Robert, 1940– . Discovering Canada.
FC25.L593 2000   j971'.009'9   C00-932565-4
F1005.L593 2000

THE CANADA COUNCIL | LE CONSEIL DES ARTS
FOR THE ARTS | DU CANADA
SINCE 1957 | DEPUIS 1957

*We acknowledge for their financial support of our
publishing program the Canada Council, the Ontario Arts
Council, and the Government of Canada through the
Book Publishing Industry Development Program (BPIDP).*

Printed and bound in Canada

Dedicated with love to
Sean and Nick

A special thanks to Diane Crew, Florence De Dominicis,
Charlette Karen, Joyce Milligan, Leslie Sutherland, and the other
librarians at the Oakville Public Library; the University of Windsor Library;
Josie Hazen; Kelly Jones; Jennifer MacKinnon; and Rene Shoemaker.

Other books in the Discovering Canada series

The Vikings

The Fur Traders

New France

Native Peoples

The Defenders

The Railways

The Loyal Refugees

Contents

There have been many rebels in Canadian history who have upset, yet influenced, its development as a nation.

Although Canadians are usually law-abiding and loyal to those in authority, our history is riddled with bloody battles and massacres that resulted from armed resistance led by fiery rebels. When threatened by violence, loyal citizens refused to be intimidated while defending the government. Most rebel causes were later accepted by Canadians through peaceful transition, not revolution.

Rebels are people who object to, question, or defy the lawful or existing authority. They resist the controls or conventions of the established society. Usually they represent a cause or a belief. The new ideas or different behaviour of rebels can shock those in authority. Some rebels fight for their cause with weapons, others with words, and others still by antisocial behaviour. Young people are often considered to be rebels, but as society changes, new ideas frequently become acceptable.

Some rebels succeed by causing changes peacefully. Others break the law, take control by force, or even kill those who don't agree with them. The United States of America was created by armed rebels who took control by deadly force.* Canadian rebels who used violence were rejected by the law-abiding citizens. A successful Canadian rebel is a person who achieves change through peaceful means, not by bloodshed. Canada was created by evolution, not by revolution.

*see the seventh book in this Discovering Canada series, *The Loyal Refugees*, for more information.

1 *Lower Canada Rebels*

Louis-Joseph Papineau and Others

In 1837, two rebellions occurred at the same time: one in Lower Canada (present-day Quebec) and the other in Upper Canada (present-day Ontario).

Louis-Joseph Papineau led the revolt against the governing party in Lower Canada. The French-speaking Reformers who sought representative government called themselves *Patriotes*.

At age 28, Papineau was elected to Lower Canada's Legislative Assembly. He soon became the leader of the Parti Canadien and Speaker of the Assembly. As was the case in the other British colonies, the assembly had no real power. The important decisions were made by the Chateau Clique, a group consisting mainly of English-speaking colonists appointed by Lord Gosford, the governor.

Frustrated by the harsh social conditions of unemployment and poverty, Papineau created a more radical party, the Parti Patriote. In 1834, he and his *Patriotes* demanded responsible government in a document called the Ninety-Two Resolutions. When their demands were refused, Papineau began a boycott of British products. He started to dress as a common habitant in homespun clothing, wearing a knitted toque and a red sash. His emotional speeches soon fueled open rebellion. Street fights between French and English youth broke out in Montreal. During a clash on November 6, 1837, one Patriote leader named Thomas Brown lost an eye.

By November 16, the rebels had gathered in armed mobs. Lord Gosford ordered the arrest of all the Patriote leaders. Papineau, disguised in a long hooded cloak, escaped from Montreal in a coach with his friend Edmund B. O'Callaghan, the editor of the pro-Patriote newspaper called the *Vindicator*. They joined with other rebel leaders in the countryside.

A troop of 20 cavalry was sent to St. John (St-Jean) where it arrested three rebel leaders, but upon its return to Montreal it was stopped by a mob of 150 Patriote farmers who rescued the captives.

Battle of St-Denis (November 23, 1837)
Wolfred Nelson, the rebel leader at St-Denis, had gathered an army of 800 Patriotes. Colonel Charles Gore was sent with five companies of troops to put down the insurrection. Papineau had taken shelter in the rebel headquarters at St-Denis, but rather than leading the army, he and O'Callaghan left town before the fighting began. The battle lasted over seven hours and the rebels, led by Nelson, were victorious. Fifty British soldiers were killed and Gore was forced to retreat. Only 13 Patriotes died.

Battle of St-Charles (November 25, 1837)
Within a few days, another British force, commanded by Colonel George Wetherall, attacked the fortified rebel barricades at St-Charles. The leader of the 400 Patriotes was Brown, who had lost an eye in the Montreal riots. Papineau and O'Callaghan arrived, gave Brown the title of General, and then disappeared. This time the British were victorious. Over 60 rebels were slaughtered and every building was burnt.

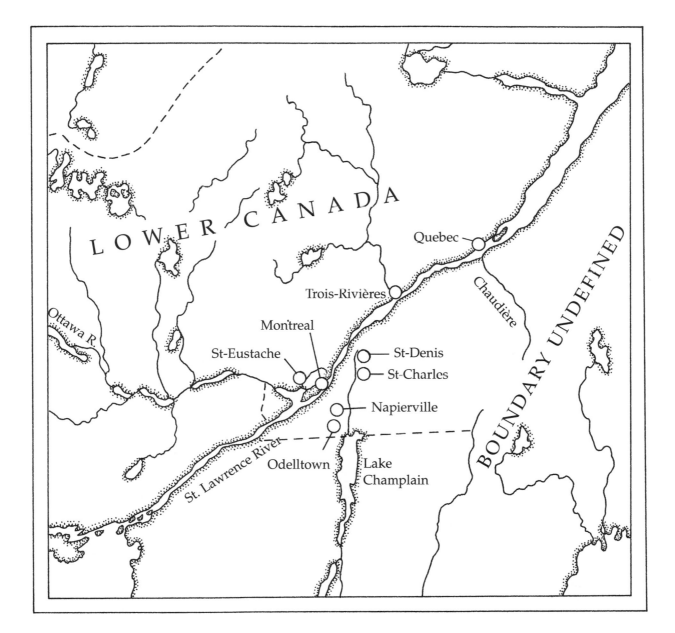

LOWER CANADA

Ottawa R.

St. Lawrence River

St-Eustache

Montreal

Trois-Rivières

Quebec

Chaudière

St-Denis

St-Charles

Napierville

Odelltown

Lake Champlain

BOUNDARY UNDEFINED

Pursuing the Patriotes

The rebellion caused hatred and led to atrocities on both sides. Jock Weir, a popular young officer in the British 32nd Regiment, was murdered and his body savagely mutilated by the Patriotes before the first battle at St-Denis. On December 2, Colonel Gore returned to St-Denis with eight companies of troops, captured the town, and destroyed the houses of the Patriote supporters. By early December, Papineau, O'Callaghan, Nelson, Brown, and other rebel leaders recognized their revolt was a failure and fled to the USA.

Battle of St-Eustache (December 14, 1837)

The remaining leaders of the reform movement were in the countryside north of Montreal. A Swiss immigrant named Amury Girod was their general at St-Eustache and his hot-headed colonel was Jean-Olivier Chénier. Supported by the loyal citizen militia, red-coated British troops descended upon them. It was clear that the armed bands of rebels in the small villages were no match for the professional British army that was pursuing them.

Girod and other rebel leaders decided to flee, but Chénier broke down and cried when his comrades told him that the situation was hopeless. The passionate rebel chose to ignore the cold facts. Instead of running for safety, he decided to fight to the death. Waving a rusty sword and shouting patriotic slogans, he prepared to defend the town of St-Eustache.

As reports on the approach of the army from Montreal grew, the numbers of the rebels at St-Eustache shrank. Chénier had forced many of them to join him by raiding neighbouring farms in search of men and boys to enlarge his army. He even captured some reluctant Patriote

supporters as they attended church services in town. Despite the protests of the priest, he took control of the church. At 11:30 a.m. on December 14, 1837, Chénier waited, surrounded by his remaining Patriotes.

Distant bugles announced the approach of the British troops. When the red-coated horsemen were spotted across the river, Chénier confidently set out on the frozen surface of the water with about 100 followers and disappeared among the scattered islands.

Shots were heard. Chénier and his men reappeared, on the run, firing as they retreated back to St-Eustache. The line of red-coated horsemen was in hot pursuit. A field gun roared and a round shot skidded across the ice into the midst of the scattering rebels.

Most of the Patriotes escaped to the countryside in disorder, but Chénier shouted above the confusion and pointed to the church, forcing the men who were ahead of him into it.

"We have no guns!" some cried. But Chénier coolly replied, "There will be dead soon; you will be able to use theirs."

Thus, the remaining 60 rebels took shelter in their "stone trap," the church of St-Eustache.

Last Stand
Colonel Wetherall, the victor at St-Charles, and his troops closed in from the north end of town and stopped at the church. With cannons, he opened fire on the front of the building. Colonel John Maitland's men moved in from the opposite direction.

The presbytery was connected to the back of the church by a covered way. Lieutenant Ned Wetherall (son of the colonel) and two other British officers crept through it to enter the church.

The Patriotes had destroyed the stairs leading to the galleries and loft where they had taken shelter. Rebel fire rained down on the three officers as they gathered together the splintered wooden remains of the stairs. They sprinkled the pile with black gun powder and struck flint to it. As the flames exploded, the trio escaped from the building.

The church was completely surrounded by infantry. Waiting with fixed bayonets at the rear of the church was the 32nd Regiment, whose officer, Jock Weir, had been murdered at St-Denis.

As the dry wood of the structure's interior blazed, the screams of the men trapped inside could be heard. Some were caught by the flames; others jumped from the windows. Those attempting to escape met a quicker death. Guns were fired at them and steel bayonets were driven into their bodies. The officers of the 32nd Regiment shouted at their troops to stop slaughtering the terrified survivors, but they were not heard over the loud battle cries of "Remember Jock Weir!"

Chénier was hit by a musket ball as he slipped through a narrow window, but he still raced to reach a ditch behind the cemetery. A second musket ball hit him in the heart. He was dead before he hit the ground.

At 6 p.m., the roof of the church caved in, but smoke continued to rise from the wreckage until the next morning. The massacre at St-Eustache ended the armed rebellion of 1837 in Lower Canada.

Chasseur Uprising (November 1838)

In 1838, the leadership of the Patriote refugees who had fled to the USA passed on to Robert Nelson, whose brother had defeated the regulars at St-Denis. Papineau and O'Callaghan objected to Nelson's tactics when he began a series of random border raids into Lower Canada from his American base.

By November, the Patriote call to arms was again echoing through the countryside as Sir John Colborne received reports that Nelson had crossed the border and amassed an armed force of 3,000 at Napierville. Nelson had organized secret military groups, known as *Les Frères Chasseurs*, throughout Lower Canada and they were waiting to rise up in revolt and join his invading force from Vermont. When Nelson arrived in November of 1838 and declared himself the President of the Canadian Republic, the Chasseurs emerged and captured towns throughout Lower Canada.

Battle of Odelltown (November 9, 1838)

Loyalists were attacked, robbed, imprisoned, and killed by the Chasseurs. Loyal volunteers and militia formed groups to defend themselves. In Odelltown, the volunteers spotted Nelson's Chasseurs descending upon them. Two hundred loyalists took shelter in the stone church. The events of the battle at St-Eustache seemed to be occurring again, but this time the rebels were the attackers. Nelson ordered the church set on fire to drive the defenders out, but more loyalists arrived. The battle at Odelltown lasted two and a half hours in the midst of blinding snow flurries. The rebels were defeated and Nelson fled back over the border. Colborne arrived with 3,300 soldiers the next day.

Meanwhile, at Chateauguay, loyal volunteers were defending themselves from Chasseurs when they heard the war whoops of Caughnawaga Natives and the screech of highland bagpipes coming to their aid. Together they recaptured the area the rebels had taken. Later, Glengarry highlanders from Upper Canada retook Beauharnois from the Chasseurs.

The 2,000 Chasseurs who had emerged at St-Denis, St-Ours, and St-Charles melted away as news of the loyalist victories reached them. The uprising of 1838 was over. The majority of the citizens in Lower Canada had rejected the practice of physical force to gain political power.

Louis LaFontaine and Lord Elgin

Louis LaFontaine was a Patriote who believed that French Canadians should rule themselves. He had supported Papineau, but refused to take up arms in rebellion. While the radicals were in exile after their revolt failed, he worked peacefully to create reforms.

In 1847, James Bruce, Earl of Elgin, was appointed governor. He believed that Canadians should rule themselves. Upper and Lower Canada became one territory. By 1848, LaFontaine and Robert Baldwin joined forces as the two premiers in the joint assembly, which was controlled by elected Reformers. La Fontaine ensured that the rebels, such as Papineau, were pardoned and allowed to return to Canada. When LaFontaine insisted that French Canadians be compensated for their losses during the rebellion, his house was destroyed by Tories and he was attacked in the streets. Nevertheless, Louis LaFontaine introduced the Rebellion Losses Bill and the Reformers supported it.

The Tories insisted that Lord Elgin use his power as governor to veto the bill. Lord Elgin refused to overrule the decision of the elected representatives and the bill passed. Reformers achieved responsible government and LaFontaine was a hero!

Burning Parliament

The Tories, outraged that the Reformers were giving money to people they considered to be traitors and rebels, threw garbage, rocks, and dead rats at Lord Elgin's carriage. A mob of 1,500 broke into Parliament House in Montreal and set it on fire. Lord Elgin refused to use force against the rioters. He calmly insisted on supporting the Reform Party, and continued as governor of Canada for the next five years.

Loyal Church

The Roman Catholic Church disapproved of the radical Patriotes. It warned that those who revolted would be refused absolution and religious burial.

Suicide

Girod, the general at St-Eustache, escaped before the battle in his *carriole* (a sleigh of the rich). Wandering aimlessly through the countryside he was stopped by loyal forces, but rather than face capture, he placed his pistol to his head and shot himself.

Louis-Joseph Papineau

Exiled

After his failed revolt, Papineau spent eight years in exile. When a pardon allowed Patriote rebels to return to Lower Canada, Papineau was re-elected to the assembly, but he soon retired quietly to a seigneury in the country.

Create Revolutionary Slogans and Banners

If you were planning a revolution or demonstration, you would need to create slogans and banners that expressed your beliefs or viewpoints.

What You Need:

markers   stapler and staples   flat wood sticks (1 metre long)
2 round poles, 2 metres long   cardboard or bristol board
cardboard or cloth/vinyl fabric (the size that you want for your slogan)

What to Do:

1. Think of a cause that will be the main objective of your revolution or demonstration. For example: Is there something that you would like to save or protect that is currently in danger? Are there some basic rights needed for a specific group of people (the homeless, children, senior citizens, the disabled, etc.)? Are there powerful groups or companies that have too much political or economic control over your life? Could you support a specific viewpoint or action to protect Canada from danger?
2. Invent slogans that express in a few words the cause that you support. For example: "Save Canada!" (how?), "Give Us Shelter!" (who?), "Self Help!" (to do what?), "Ban Junk Food!" (or cigarettes, alcohol, etc.), "Give Kids the Vote!" (why?). You may wish to include visual symbols on your banners (a maple leaf, a beaver, etc.).
3. Construct banners on which you can state your slogans or beliefs. (Use the instructions on the following page to build your banners.)

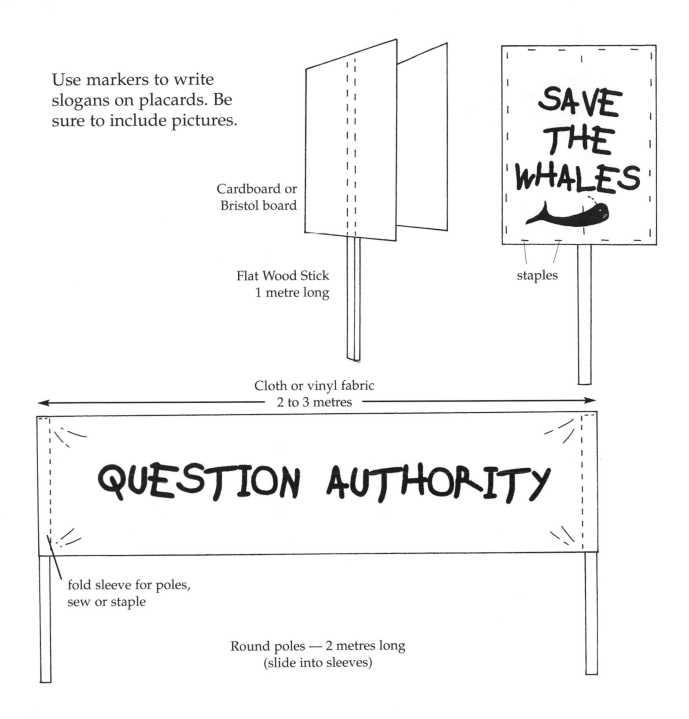

Use markers to write slogans on placards. Be sure to include pictures.

Cardboard or Bristol board

Flat Wood Stick 1 metre long

SAVE THE WHALES

staples

Cloth or vinyl fabric
2 to 3 metres

QUESTION AUTHORITY

fold sleeve for poles, sew or staple

Round poles — 2 metres long
(slide into sleeves)

2 *Upper Canada Rebels*

William Lyon Mackenzie and Others

At the same time as the Patriotes in Lower Canada were revolting, another rebellion was erupting in Upper Canada (present-day Ontario).

William Lyon Mackenzie, a Scottish settler, was the leader of the Reform movement. He was seeking an American-style revolution in Upper Canada where the governing clique, led by another Scotsman, John Strachan, was known as the Family Compact. When Mackenzie's newspaper, the *Colonial Advocate*, published critical assaults on the governing elite (years before the rebellion), Tory vandals swarmed into his offices in York (later to be renamed Toronto). They overturned desks, scattered papers, and destroyed his printing press. After demolishing the building, they threw the contents into the bay.

The destruction resulted in a lawsuit that not only awarded Mackenzie enough money in damages to build a new printing press, but the event also made him a popular Reform hero. He was elected to the Legislative Assembly of Upper Canada in 1828.

The governor of Upper Canada, Sir Francis Bond Head, was appointed by the British government. He chose his Legislative Council from the wealthy and influential members of the colony. Reformers, such as Mackenzie, could be elected to the assembly, but their decisions could be vetoed by the Legislative Council. They had no real power. The wealthy ruled, and they ruled in favour of their own business interests.

In 1831, the zealous, outspoken Mackenzie was expelled from the assembly. When the people re-elected him with more than 99 percent of the votes, he paraded victoriously through the streets of York, accompanied by bagpipes. Mackenzie was re-elected to the assembly five times, and each time he was expelled. In 1834, he was elected the first mayor of Toronto.

Reform Majority

In 1835, Mackenzie was again elected to the assembly. By this time, there was a majority of elected Reformers. In an attempt to bring about change legally, Mackenzie and others presented the Seventh Report of the Committee on Grievances.

In 1836, Governor Sir Francis Bond Head dissolved the unruly assembly. Then, in favour of the Tories, he began a personal and bitter campaign against the Reformers. Tory election posters accused the Reformers of lying and attempting to turn Canada into another American republic. The Tories won the election; even Mackenzie was defeated.

Taking Up Arms

Enraged by the interference of the British governor, Mackenzie and his associates gave up on peaceful reform. They began to hold secret meetings in private homes. They formed local committees. In the countryside, farmers practiced military drills. In November 1837, Mackenzie distributed revolutionary handbills. The rebels were training 5,000 volunteers.

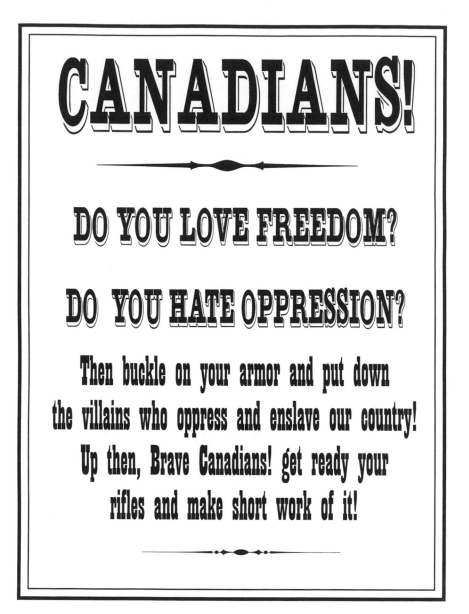

The handbill distributed by William Lyon Mackenzie in 1837

Sir Francis Bond Head

Sir Francis had sent his regular British troops to help suppress the Patriote uprising in Lower Canada. With reports of rebellion in Upper Canada, he authorized the formation of a militia regiment commanded by Colonel James FitzGibbon, a hero of the War of 1812.*

The rebellion had been set for December 7, 1837, but at the last minute the date was moved ahead to December 4. The result was confusion. Rather than the expected 5,000 rebels, only 500 gathered to attack Toronto.

* see the fifth book in this Discovering Canada series, *The Defenders*, for more information.

Montgomery's Tavern

On that cold December Monday, small groups of rebels (armed with pitchforks, clubs, old rifles, and muskets) marched along Yonge Street to gather at Montgomery's Tavern, the headquarters of the rebel forces. The building was within five kilometres of the government offices in Toronto.

The rebels set up roadblocks on Yonge Street. Colonel Robert Moodie, a government loyalist, attempted to enter Toronto to warn the governor of the rebellion. Stopped by a rebel at one of the roadblocks, Moodie fired his pistol, but was killed by the return fire, becoming the first casualty of the revolt.

24

As Mackenzie led a force of rebels toward Toronto, he encountered Alderman John Powell. The latter drew his pistol and fired point-blank into Mackenzie's face, but his weapon misfired. Powell was taken prisoner. Later that day, after killing Captain Anthony Anderson (one of the rebel leaders), Powell escaped to warn Sir Francis of the insurrection.

On the evening of Tuesday, December 8, on the spot where Maple Leaf Gardens was later built, the rebel force of 500 encountered Sheriff William Botsford Jarvis and 27 men from the Queen's York Rangers. Shots were exchanged. Not realizing that the defending force was so small, the rebels retreated back to Montgomery's Tavern.

By Thursday, both sides had reorganized. The main conflict exploded south of Montgomery's Tavern. Musket balls, bullets, and cannon shots transformed the peaceful countryside into a deadly inferno covered by thick, black smoke. Many died on both sides. Men lay bleeding along the roadside. When loyalist cannon shots hit the tavern, the rebels scattered to the north. In less than half an hour the battle was over.

Montgomery's Tavern was burnt to the ground. Mackenzie escaped to the USA, but 60 captured rebels, tied to a long rope, were paraded down Yonge Street, led by highland pipers and guarded by 600 loyal militiamen.

Second Rebellion

Later that December of 1837, a second revolt took place in the London District of Upper Canada. Dr. Charles Duncombe, the leader, was assisted by the aggressive Eliakim Malcolm from the town of Scotland and Quaker Joshua Doan from Sparta in Yarmouth Township. Doan led a rebel band known as Doan's Spartan Rangers. The rebel plan was to capture Brantford first and then march on to Hamilton.

Colonel Allan McNab commanded the loyal volunteers who captured Duncombe's deserted headquarters at Scotland. He pursued the rebels, and on December 16, he took 500 rebel prisoners at Sodom.

Navy Island

In the meantime, Mackenzie had escaped to Buffalo where he joined forces with a Dutchman from New York named Rensselaer Van Rensselaer. The latter's aim was to break the British monarchy's hold across the border in Canada. By offering promises of adventure and free land grants to unemployed Americans, they formed a liberation army of 25,000 and called themselves the Patriot Army of the North-West. On December 14, 1837, they occupied Navy Island, an island located in Canadian waters about five kilometres upstream from Niagara Falls. It became their headquarters. Mackenzie proclaimed himself Chairman of the New Republican State of Upper Canada. He even designed a flag for his new state.

Van Rensselaer appointed "Pirate Bill" Johnson as the Admiral of the Patriot Navy in the East. "Pirate Bill," born at Trois-Rivières in 1782, was the son of United Empire Loyalists, but he was anti-British. Using hideouts in the Thousand Islands, his galley attacked Canadian ships.

About 450 invaders gathered on Navy Island, land that was visible from the town of Chippawa on the Canadian side of the river. From Navy Island, Mackenzie conducted bloody raids on towns along the Canadian border. Chippawa soon became the headquarters of McNab's loyalist volunteers. Gunfire became common between the rebels on the island and the volunteers on the mainland. Men were killed on both sides.

Mackenzie's
Flag

The *Caroline*

Mackenzie was using a 26-tonne steamer, the *Caroline*, to bring supplies from the New York side of the river to his rebel force on Navy Island. Andrew Drew was the captain and commander of the loyalist naval force. He and 50 eager volunteers rowed out on December 29 armed with guns, boarding pikes, and cutlasses prepared to capture the *Caroline*. When they did not find the *Caroline* at Navy Island, they proceeded to the mainland in New York State where they discovered the vessel.

Drew, waving a sword, was one of the first to board the boat. A gun battle erupted; men were wounded and killed. The *Caroline* was captured, towed out into the river, and set on fire. As it drifted downriver toward the mighty Niagara Falls, it ran aground on the rocks. There it broke into pieces, some of which plunged over the Falls. The capture and destruction of the *Caroline*, an American ship within USA territory, outraged the Americans.

Reinforcements

Regular troops from New Brunswick and Nova Scotia arrived in Upper Canada to join the newly incorporated militia. The rebels on Navy Island retreated to New York, and on January 15, 1838, the Upper Canadian Militia occupied the island without any resistance.

The Hunters

After their rebellion failed, rebel leaders (such as Mackenzie, Duncombe, and Malcolm) and their followers flooded into the United States of America looking for shelter and assistance. Many Americans felt that they should help the Canadian rebels overthrow the British authorities so that Canada could become an independent republic like the USA.

Secret societies known as Hunters' Lodges were formed in the USA. Their members planned strategies on how to make Canada a republic. Tens of thousands of American Republicans joined the Hunters and formed the Republican Government of Upper Canada. Their commander in chief was brigadier general Lucius V. Bierce of the Ohio militia. They assumed that all Canadian citizens yearned for freedom from the British.

Loyal Volunteers

The truth was that the loyal volunteers and militia in Upper Canada were the main reason that the rebellions had failed. The Americans did not understand that the majority of Canadians opposed violent rebellion and preferred peaceful negotiation while attempting to achieve democracy.

Back in Canada, it was the loyal leaders of the militia and volunteers whom the citizens admired and followed. John Prince was the militia commander on the Detroit frontier. Colonel William Chisholm of Oakville and his Dragoons also hunted for rebels. William "Tiger" Dunlop from the

Windsor — Detroit border 1838

Huron district led an unofficial militia known as the "Invincibles" or "Huron Braves." Along the St. Lawrence River at Kingston, Colonel Richard Bonnycastle led the Frontenac and Addington militiamen.

Fighting Island (February 1838)

On February 24, rebel leader Charles Duncombe returned to Canada and occupied Fighting Island with about 150 Republicans. John Prince and his Canadian volunteers attacked and sent the invaders scrambling back to the American mainland.

Pelee Island (March 1838)

On March 3, Van Rensselaer led a force of about 400 American Republicans across the border at Pelee Island. The invaders were defeated by Canadian volunteers, and Van Rensselaer was killed.

The Short Hills (June 1838)
An Irish Roman Catholic from Pennsylvania named James Morreau led a small force of Hunters. They set up camp in the tamarack swamp in the Short Hills, south of St. Catharines. They attacked a detachment of Queen's Lancers at the town of St. John. Local militia and native warriors tracked down the invaders, who were later captured, tried, and sentenced for life to the penal colony in Australia.

Battle of the Windmill (November 1838)
Nils Gustaf Von Schoultz, a Finn of Swedish extraction living in New York, led a border attack against Fort Wellington and the town of Prescott. He and his attackers landed at Windmill Point and occupied the six-storey

windmill, which stood on a bluff above the St. Lawrence River. The invaders flew a blue silk patriot flag which read "Liberated by the Onondaga Hunters" from the top of the windmill.

Local militiamen; the 83rd and 93rd Regiments of Foot; and the Royal Navy, Marines, and Artillery bombarded the walls and captured 159 invaders. The prisoners had to be protected from angry mobs of Canadian citizens who were not interested in being "liberated." Eleven of the Hunter leaders, including Von Schoultz, were tried in Kingston and later hung. Sixty of their followers were sent to the penal colony at Van Diemen's Land. Thirty-nine teenagers were convicted and then pardoned due to their ages. They were sent back to New York.

Battle of Windsor (December 1838)

In early December, Lucius V. Bierce crossed the Canadian border with about 300 Hunters, attacked the village of Windsor, and burnt the military barracks. John Prince's volunteers and militia arrived from Sandwich. They captured 44 of the invaders and pushed the others back over the border. Six of the prisoners were sentenced to death.

American Prisoner

President Martin Van Buren issued a proclamation that Americans who attacked Canada would not be protected if captured.

Because Mackenzie was attacking Canada from the USA, the American government arrested and imprisoned him for a breach of the neutrality laws. After his release, he lived for 12 years in the USA where he wrote anti-British newspaper articles.

When an amnesty was declared in 1849, Mackenzie returned and was elected to the Legislative Assembly of Canada. By this time, the leadership of the Reform movement had been taken over by others. He eventually retired from politics and died peacefully in Toronto on August 28, 1861.

Black Loyalists

Black volunteers were strongly loyal to Canada (and therefore opposed an American-style rebellion) because they knew that slavery still existed in the USA in 1837. In Upper Canada slavery had been illegal since 1793.

The first of many black companies of volunteers was from Hamilton and was led by a white officer, Captain William Allen. The Reverend Josiah Henson from Windsor commanded another company that defended

32

Amherstburg. Henson, a black man, inspired Harriot Beecher Stowe to write *Uncle Tom's Cabin*.

Disguised as a Woman

Before the battle at Montgomery's Tavern, Mackenzie, in outlaw fashion, held up a mail coach. When the rebellion was later lost, he disguised himself in some women's clothing that had been part of the plunder from the mail coach and escaped to Buffalo in the USA.

Rebel Defender

When Von Schoultz and his followers were captured at the Battle of the Windmill, they were defended in a Kingston court by a young lawyer, John A. Macdonald, who later became the first prime minister of Canada.

Female Spy

There were many spies on both sides during the rebellions in 1837 and 1838. One rebel spy was Eunice Whiting. She was later sent to the Kingston Penitentiary for stealing a horse.

Rebel Exodus

Samuel Edison, a 33-year-old innkeeper from Upper Canada, was typical of many Canadian rebels who fled to the USA after the rebellion had failed. His son Thomas, the famous inventer, was later born at Milan, Ohio, in 1847.

Publish a Newspaper or Web Page

Many of the Canadian rebels discussed in this book (such as William Lyon Mackenzie, Amor de Cosmos, Joseph Howe, Thomas D'Arcy McGee, etc.) began their careers as newspaper publishers. Try publishing your own newspaper or create a web page newsletter about Canadian rebels. Create one alone or with the help of friends or classmates.

What You Need:
>   paper
>   pencil or pen (or typewriter or computer)
>   visuals of the personalities and events (sketches or photographs found in books or on the internet. Be sure to credit your sources.)
>   a strong opinion about the personalities and events of the 1800s

What to Do:
Use a current newspaper or web page as a guide.
1. Create a Front Page.
   Imagine that you are back in the 1800s. Write news stories as they might have appeared at that time. Use sketches or photographs that illustrate the stories. Try to be creative when inventing your headlines. A news story should supply answers to the following questions: *What* happened? *When* did it happen? *Where* did it happen? *Who* was involved? *Why* did it happen or have the outcome that it did?

2. Create an Editorial Page.

   As the editor, this is where you include your opinion on the issues of the time. What does the editor think about the rebels and their actions? The editorial page might also include Letters to the Editor in which readers can express their viewpoints on issues or on the events of the day. Encourage others to participate in your newspaper or web page by publishing their viewpoints. If you have cartooning talents, a political cartoon of the times might also be included on this page. You should be able to find actual political cartoons from the 1800s through your public library and the internet.

3. Create a Sports Page.

   Investigate the sporting events of the 1800s and write a review of them. For example: In 1867, a rowing team called the St. John Four from St. John, New Brunswick, won the first international athletic victory for the new nation of Canada; or there's Louis Cyr, from Quebec, who was known as the "Strongest Man Who Ever Lived."

4. Create Advertisements.

   What advertisements might have appeared in the 1800s? What goods would be for sale? Weapons? Clothing? Furniture? Food? Horses?

5. Create Feature Stories.

   What kinds of stories about rebel personalities and events might have been written back in the 1800s? If web pages existed back then, what kinds of stories might have appeared?

Thomas D'Arcy McGee and Others.

In the United States of America, the Irish brotherhood known as the Fenians was led by John J. O'Neill, who called himself a general. The Fenians encouraged all Irishmen to overthrow British rule, in Ireland or in Canada.

On June 2, 1866, O'Neill led 800 Irish American soldiers across the Niagara River and captured Fort Erie, Ontario. He hoped to unite Irish Canadians and others into revolting against the British control of the colonies, but loyal Canadians quickly grabbed their weapons and forced him back over the border. The American government hesitated to take action against the powerful Fenian brotherhood, which had 15,000 angry, hostile members.

Next, O'Neill prepared for an invasion of the Eastern Townships of Quebec. He amassed three million rounds of ammunition in his headquarters at Franklin, Vermont. On May 25, 1870, he attacked Ecles Hill, but the Canadian militia, proud of their new Dominion of Canada created in 1867, beat him back again. He was finally jailed by the American government.

Young Rebel

As a teenager, Thomas D'Arcy McGee was a dedicated fighter for an independent Ireland and was very anti-British. At age 17, he immigrated to

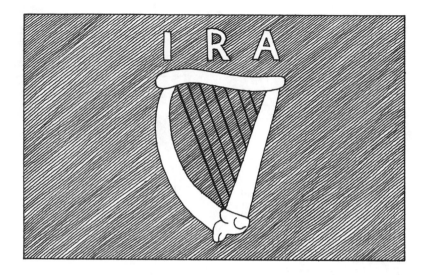

Fenian
Flag

North America and joined the staff of the Boston *Pilot*. By the time he was 19, he had become its editor. McGee had already proven himself to be an outstanding orator, newspaper editor, and poet. He married in 1847 and eventually had five daughters and one son.

His fame as a newspaper person and lecturer led to his return to Ireland to work for the *Freeman's Journal* and *The Nation*. He became involved in the attempted rebellion of 1848 and had to flee Ireland, disguised as a priest. Returning to the USA, he published an article that blamed the Irish clergy for the rebellion's failure and signed his article "Thomas D'Arcy McGee, A Traitor to the British Government."

Back in the USA, McGee became less radical. Extreme Irish Republicans often verbally attacked him over his more conservative political views as a mere Reformer.

In 1857, Thomas D'Arcy McGee moved to Montreal and started a

newspaper called the *New Era*. He was a short man and his shoulders were stooped. His fringe of beard ran from ear to ear, and his head was topped with an unruly mop of hair. McGee later began a new career, that of politician. Within one year, he was elected to the Legislative Assembly of Canada for Montreal West.

British North America Act

McGee, the former rebel, became known as the "silver-tongued orator," of Confederation. His passionate speeches were a major force in helping an independent Canada to form from a peaceful union of the former British colonies. The union was established by the British North America Act (BNA Act). McGee was Sir John A. Macdonald's right-hand man, and one of the most important Fathers of Confederation. He was present at Charlottetown as well as Quebec when the new Dominion of Canada was being formed.

He declared, "As fragments we shall be lost; but let us be united and we shall be as a rock."

The Fenian rebels opposed McGee and his efforts to create an independent Canadian nation that would remain loyal to Britain. In the first election for the new House of Commons in 1867, his opponent was Bernard Devlon, an Irish extremist.

McGee lashed out at his powerful adversaries. "As to Fenianism, I have strangled it when it first attempted to concentrate in Canada and I am not going to be annoyed by its carcass." He bravely, or foolishly, ignored their threats. "I have been told that if I would let the Fenians alone, I would be left alone. But I drove the man from me."

Assassination

Patrick James Whelan, a Fenian who had worked for Devlon during the election, swore he would "blow his (McGee's) bloody brains out!"

Late at night on April 6, 1868, Whelan was in the visitors' gallery of the House of Commons. He was stalking up and down, and shaking his fist at McGee, who was below with the other members of the House.

After midnight, McGee stopped in front of his boardinghouse on Sparks Street in Ottawa to unlock the door. He was shot from behind with a 6-shot Smith & Wesson revolver. The gun was owned by Whelan, who later insisted he was innocent, but bragged that he knew who had shot McGee. However, Whelan refused to reveal the name of the murderer and was hanged for the assassination. Experts agree that the assassination had been ordered by the Fenians.

At age 42, Thomas D'Arcy McGee, the rebel-turned-peaceful-Reformer, became a Canadian hero and martyr.

Premonition of Death

Strangely enough, a childhood premonition led Thomas D'Arcy McGee to write a poem entitled "Forewarned," that described his own assassination.

> In the time of my boyhood I had a strange feeling,
> That I was to die in the noon of my day,
> Not quietly into the silent grave stealing,
> But torn like a blasted oak, suddenly away.

Loyal Citizens

Loyal citizens who had formed militia units to support the British forces came from all sorts of ethnic origins. Scottish Highlanders, Jews, Poles, Germans, Aboriginals, Africans, and Irish Roman Catholics, as well as many French Canadians took up arms against the rebels.

First and Last

Many presidents and politicians in the USA have been assassinated; many attempts have been made unsuccessfully on others. The assassination of Thomas D'Arcy McGee was the first and last of a Canadian federal politician. More than 100 years later, a Quebec politician named Pierre Laporte became the second politician to be assassinated in Canada. He was murdered by radical French separatists.

Public Execution

The last Canadian execution the public witnessed was that of Patrick James Whelan on February 11, 1869. After that, executions were performed in private with only official witnesses in attendance. For many years now, Canada has not practiced capital punishment. No one is executed in Canada today, regardless of the crime that was committed.

4 *Political Rebels*

Joseph Howe, Amor de Cosmos, and Others

Political rebels who became Reformers frequently began their careers as newspaper editors who criticized the lack of fair or representative government in their colonies or provinces.

Red-haired Joseph Howe was born in Halifax, Nova Scotia, on December 13, 1804. Joseph's family was very poor; the boy had to leave school when he was only 13 years old because there was no money to allow him to continue. (At that time in history, there were no laws to ensure that children received an education and there was no financial aid for poor families.) He began to work in a printing office.

Howe saved his money. At the age of 23, his love of reading and writing led him to buy a partnership in a newspaper, the *Acadian*. By 1828, he owned his own newspaper, the *Novascotian*.

Freedom of the Press

Nova Scotia was governed by the dictatorial Council of Twelve. When Joseph published a letter that accused the magistrates of Halifax of "incompetence, neglect and corruption in administrating the law," he was immediately charged with libel. No lawyer would defend him against the powerful British-appointed authorities, so in court he argued his own case for freedom of the press.

After an emotional six-hour speech that caused one jury member to break into tears, Howe concluded, "Yes, gentlemen, come what will, while I live, Nova Scotia shall have the blessing of an open and unshackled press."

When Howe was acquitted, the citizens of Halifax exploded into a spontaneous celebration that turned into a two-day holiday of rejoicing in the streets. Joseph Howe was a hero.

His new popularity as a Reformer brought him trouble and enemies. One opponent charged into his newspaper office on horseback, waving a sword. As windows were smashed into the street, Howe pulled the man from the horse and disarmed him. Other enemies challenged him to deadly duels. He fought two with pistols before refusing others. He claimed, "A live editor is more useful than a dead hero."

To bring about reform, Howe entered politics and was elected as a representative of the Legislative Assembly in 1836. As leader of the Reformers, he fought for 11 years to obtain responsible government. He forced the governor, Lord Viscount Falkland, to be recalled to England, and by 1847 a system of responsible government was established in Nova Scotia.

Unlike Upper and Lower Canada, there was no armed rebellion in Nova Scotia under the peaceful leadership of Joseph Howe. He held the position of premier of the province from 1860 to 1863.

Seeking Adventure

Joseph Howe was a hero to young Bill Smith (William Alexander Smith) who was born in Windsor, Nova Scotia, in 1825. At age 14, Billy was working in a grocery store in Halifax when stories of the fabulous gold discoveries in California reached his ears.

Years later, Bill decided to leave home to seek adventure and wealth in the Wild West. He joined a covered wagon train for most of the long and dangerous trip across the wide continent. Along the way they were attacked by Aboriginals defending their territory from white settlers. But that wasn't Bill's only challenge, he also had to defend himself from a group of Mormon women in the wagon train who collectively, as was their custom, wished to become his wives. (Marriage, however, was not one of his goals in life; he would remain a bachelor until his death.)

Alone on horseback, Bill finally arrived in California. The lean Nova Scotian, with blazing eyes and a curly black beard, wore twin revolvers sticking out of his boot tops as he strutted through the California goldfields. He was unsuccessful as a gold miner and he turned to a new novelty, photography. He made a living by taking pictures of miners and their claims. He soon had a reputation as being a drinker and partier.

In 1854, Bill Smith changed his name by legislative decree to the flamboyant Amor de Cosmos, which means "Lover of the Universe."

Northern Gold Rush

In 1858 gold was discovered in the Fraser River, and thousands of Americans rushed north to the British settlements on the West Coast of North America. In 1855, there were fewer than 800 European settlers on Vancouver Island and only a handful of fur traders on the mainland. The discovery of gold brought 30,000 fortune-seeking immigrants to the area.

From one shipload of Californian adventurers stepped a passenger who would change the lives of everyone in the colony and become the most controversial figure in British Columbia. The stranger, Amor de Cosmos, was impeccably dressed with top hat, formal coat, and walking cane as he swaggered arrogantly ashore.

Port of Nanaimo

British Columbia

Since 1821, the Hudson's Bay Company had ruled the British settlement. The swarms of newcomers to the region were a threat to the fur trade and the authority of the Hudson's Bay Company's governor.

Like Joseph Howe (his idol back in Nova Scotia), Amor de Cosmos founded a newspaper, the *British Columnist*, and through it began to fight for responsible government. The newspaper attacked the governor of

Vancouver Island, James Douglas. The enraged Douglas swore "to muzzle the meddlesome, eccentric newcomer." The governor used an ancient British law to demand the huge fee of $3,000 for a newspaper license. Amor was unable to pay the fee and went to jail. The citizens regarded him as a popular hero and Douglas as a villain. Within days, they raised the bond money and subscriptions to the paper multiplied, allowing it to publish three times a week instead of just once.

Amor de Cosmos accused Douglas of being "an unsuccessful statesman and traitor to his country." Douglas called Amor de Cosmos "a self-styled Reformer who wrote as though half mad." A very erratic individual, Amor de Cosmos would not only attack opponents in his newspaper, but at times, would engage them in physical fights on the streets.

In 1863, the radical Amor de Cosmos entered politics and was elected to the Vancouver Island House of Assembly. He immediately proposed that the island be politically united with the British Columbian mainland, which eventually occurred in 1866. Amor de Cosmos next caused turmoil by suggesting that British Columbia become part of a new union, far to the east, called Canada. Most of the new citizens were from the United States of America and wanted B.C. to become part of the USA. In 1871, Amor de Cosmos' second dream became a reality when B.C. was named the sixth Canadian province.

Amor de Cosmos was elected not only to the federal House of Commons in Ottawa but also to the provincial assembly where he became the premier of British Columbia. As premier, he locked the British-appointed governor-general out of his position in cabinet, claiming that the latter's presence was a threat to responsible government.

Fort St. James

BRITISH
COLUMBIA

ALBERTA

Fraser
River

Campbell
River

VANCOUVER
ISLAND

Kamloops

Nanaimo

Vancouver
Fort Langley

Victoria

CANADA
USA

Amor de Cosmos

Pacific Scandal

In Ottawa, Amor de Cosmos insisted that the Canadian government honour its promise to build a railway to the West Coast. In the agreement of union, B.C. was guaranteed that the railway would be completed within 10 years, but an incident known as the "Pacific Scandal" had halted the railroad construction. Amor de Cosmos led a B.C. delegation to London, England, threatening to withdraw from Confederation. He forced the Canadian government to complete the transcontinental railway by 1885.*

Death in Insane Asylum

In 1882, Amor de Cosmos was defeated in an election. During the last years of his life, he became a pitiful character, wandering the streets of Victoria, gaunt and hawk-like, still dressed in formal attire. Eventually, he was judged to be insane and locked away in a mental institution where he died in July of 1897.

* see the sixth book in this Discovering Canada series, *The Railways*, for more information.

Sad Funeral

Although he had brought responsible government to the northern West Coast, created British Columbia, and ensured that Canada became a nation from coast to coast, Amor de Cosmos' death went unnoticed and unmourned by the public. An old political rival who attended the funeral was shocked and wrote a letter to the editor of the local newspaper.

At the graveyard some 20 or 30 saw the casket lowered. This was the mockery of honour paid to Amor de Cosmos, whom 40 years ago a large proportion of the people considered a hero, a patriot, who fought for the emancipation of the people.

Sir James Douglas

Black Rebel

Mary Ann Shadd Carey, a black woman, used the newspaper that she founded in Windsor, Ontario, the *Provincial Freeman*, to write about and fight for integration.

Punctuation Rebel!

Ma Murray, the flamboyant editor of the *Alaska Highway News*, was so notorious for her poor grammar that she would publish a paragraph of punctuation marks once a year for her readers to "sprinkle as they wished" on her writing.

Traitor?

In 1867, Joseph Howe rejected the plans of his political opponent, Charles Tupper, to join the Canadian Confederation. Howe travelled to England to try to stop the British government from passing the British North America Act, but he failed. Nevertheless, he did persuade easterners to reject Confederation and was still attempting to have the BNA Act repealed when Sir John A. Macdonald and Thomas D'Arcy McGee arranged to meet with him. Those two great men persuaded Howe that Confederation would mean "better terms" for Nova Scotia. When convinced of the advantages and necessity of Confederation, Howe changed his opinion. Many former supporters of Howe considered him to be a traitor when he changed sides to support the Canadian Confederation.

Construct an Electronic Board Game

You can construct your own Electronic Board Game designed to test a player's knowledge about Canadian rebels.

What You Need:
electric wire
battery holder
2 C batteries
a light bulb or buzzer with electrical connections
thick cardboard (or thin wood) (about 50 cm by 100 cm)
a drill or a pair of scissors
paper
glue
pencil or pen (typewriter or computer)

Note: Your wire cables, battery holder, and light bulb (or buzzer) will have to have connections to create a simple electrical circuit. Use the diagram of the Electronic Board Game on page 57 as a guide.

CAUTION: When working with electricity, it is wise to have adult supervision. Also, electricity can cause a fire, so if you are using paper and cardboard, please be careful.

Construct an Electronic Board Game

What to Do:

1. Select 10 Canadian rebels.
2. Write a short description (in the form of a question) that would identify each rebel.

For example: In 1916, who forced the Manitoba government to allow women to vote? (Nellie McClung); Who led the Chasseur Uprising of 1838? (Robert Nelson); Who was elected as the first mayor of Toronto? (William Lyon Mackenzie).

3. Glue the 10 names of the rebels down the left-hand side of the board. Drill or cut a hole beside each name.
4. Mix the rebels' descriptions up so that they are **not** beside the names that they represent and then glue the descriptions of the rebels down the right-hand side of the board. Drill or cut a hole beside each description.
5. Connect two long pieces of electric wire between the battery holder and light bulb (or buzzer) in a simple circuit, so that when you touch the ends of the wires together, they cause the bulb to light (or the buzzer to sound).
6. On the back of the board, use pieces of electric wire to connect the names of the rebels to the correct description. Allow a piece of the wire to show through the holes that you drilled on the front of the board.
7. When you touch the ends of the wire to the matching name and description on the front of your board, it should complete your electrical circuit and cause the light to go on (or the buzzer to sound). This will indicate to the player that he or she has selected the correct match of rebel to the description.
8. Add colours or designs to your board to make it attractive.

Construct an Electronic Board Game

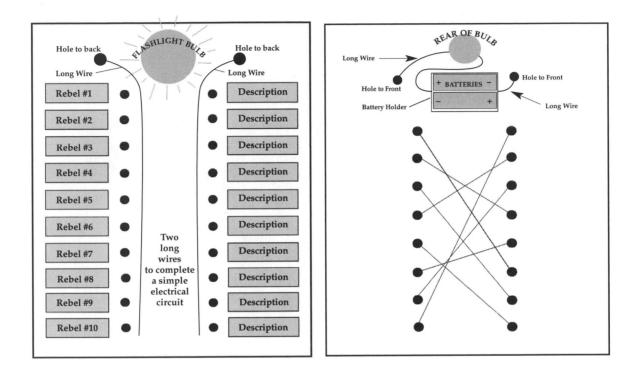

FRONT OF BOARD   REAR OF BOARD

5 *Aboriginal Rebels*

Louis Riel, Gabriel Dumont, Big Bear, and Others

As the new country of Canada expanded westward, it encountered new obstacles and rebels.

In January 1869, the powerful Hudson's Bay Company was persuaded to sell much of its land in the northwest to the Canadian government for 300,000 pounds.

The inhabitants of the Red River settlement were not consulted or even informed of the sale. The Canadian government appointed William McDougall as lieutenant governor of the new colony, replacing Governor Alexander McTavish of the Hudson's Bay Company. On Thursday, November 2, 1869, suspicious and outraged Métis rebelled against the sale. (Métis is the term used to describe a person of part Native Canadian and part European heritage.)

Red River Rebellion

The rumours of a possible rebellion ran through the nearby village of Winnipeg in advance of the invasion. Terror gripped some of the Canadians who had just arrived from the east. A Métis army was marching toward Fort Garry, the Hudson's Bay Company post at the juncture of the Red and Assiniboine rivers. The armed mob of 120 burst through the open, unguarded gates and occupied the fort without any resistance.

Their leader was Louis Riel, a Métis born on October 22, 1844, in St. Boniface. Louis was a good student so, at age 13, he was sent by Bishop

Lower Fort Garry

Taché to Montreal to study to become a priest. Discovering that he was not suited to the religious life, Riel returned to Manitoba.

On November 16, 1869, the Métis created *Le Comité National des Métis de la Rivière Rouge*. John Bruce was president; Louis Riel was secretary. They refused to allow McDougall inside the occupied Fort Garry because his duties as governor did not officially begin until December.

Eight days later, they issued a bill of rights for the colony. All was peaceful. Riel, the passionate orator, was elected president when John Bruce resigned. Riel ruled the captured settlement for months as he bargained with the Canadian government for Manitoba's entry into the Canadian Confederation.

When a settler from Ontario named Thomas Scott attempted to overthrow the Métis rebels, he was jailed. When Scott continued to defy Riel, he was executed on March 4, 1870.

By May, the Red River Rebellion was a political success. Ottawa guaranteed the rights of the people of Manitoba in the new union with Canada. But when Colonel Garnet Wolseley, the new governor, arrived with a few hundred aggressive troops, Louis Riel fled to the USA because of the price on his head.

Although he was now an outlaw, the people regarded Louis Riel as a hero and called him "The Father of Manitoba." They elected him in 1874 to the Parliament of Canada. However, when Louis arrived in Ottawa, he was expelled from the House of Commons and banished from Canada for five years. He lived for the next 15 years in exile.

Louis' personality changed drastically. He spent two years in insane asylums, changed his name to the biblical "David," and married. Louis came to regard himself as a prophet and waited for his people to recall him to serve them.

Prince of the Plains

Gabriel Dumont, known as the "Prince of the Plains," was born in 1838 in Saskatchewan. Both his parents were Métis, and he grew up hunting buffalo on fast ponies called "buffalo runners."

Dumont was famous among his people and was the youngest person elected to lead the great buffalo hunt. He was a born leader, and it was said he possessed the gift of healing wounds.

As the railway and settlers from the east invaded the Prairies, the Métis saw the buffalo herds that they and the prairie Natives depended on for food and clothing begin to disappear. Concerned about their survival,

Gabriel Dumont

the Métis wanted protection for their lands and the legal titles to their farms on the South Saskatchewan River. Their concerns were ignored by Ottawa.

Gabriel and three other Métis leaders decided to travel south to Montana in the USA. They wanted to urge Louis Riel, the man who had guaranteed the rights of the people of Manitoba in the new Confederation of Canada, to lead their cause.

In June of 1884, Riel was a schoolteacher in Montana. He enthusiastically greeted the four grim, dusty Métis who had just ridden 1,000 kilometres from Saskatchewan. Riel knelt and offered thanks to God because he believed that the enslaved people had sent for their "David."

Riel returned to Canada and attempted peaceful negotiations. When Ottawa ignored him, the Métis declared a provisional government.

North-West Rebellion (1885)

Rebellion exploded when 200 Métis attacked a force of 56 North West Mounted Police (NWMP) and 41 loyal volunteers at Duck Lake, Saskatchewan. One of the first shots killed Gabriel Dumont's younger brother and a bullet from a Snider rifle cut a path through Gabriel's own skull, leaving a permanent silver streak in his long, black hair.

In the confusion of the battle, an unarmed figure in a flowing black robe was waving a cross. It was Louis Riel. He rode through the bullets, urging his people onward. The Mounties, under the command of Major Leif Newry Fitzroy Crozier, were forced to retreat. As his enemies fled in disorder, Dumont wanted to pursue them and kill the survivors. But Riel objected to more bloodshed, and Dumont, his lieutenant general, obediently restrained his sharpshooting buffalo hunters. Twelve North West Mounted Police officers were killed at Duck Lake, as were five Métis.

The next days were full of violence. Sir John A. Macdonald sent 8,000 troops under General Frederick Dobson Middleton to quell the North-West Rebellion. As the soldiers approached Fish Creek, Dumont attacked the superior force that was armed with cannons and new weapons called Gatling guns.

The Métis guerrillas dug in at Batoche. After three days of fierce fighting against overwhelming odds, they ran out of ammunition. They were forced to shoot nails, stones, and metal buttons in place of bullets.

After they were defeated at Batoche, Gabriel Dumont fled to the USA. Louis Riel wandered aimlessly through the wilderness for days before he

decided to surrender. He was tried for treason in Regina. The rebel Louis
Riel was found guilty and hanged on the gallows.

Native Rebels

Most of the Native Peoples in the west chose to accept the western expan-
sion of the railways and new settlers.

Crowfoot, a Blackfoot chief, negotiated, with the assistance of his
trusted friend Father Albert Lacombe, to allow the Canadian Pacific Railway to cross his territory. Chief Sitting Bull of the Sioux also avoided
violence and bloodshed by using peaceful dialogue.

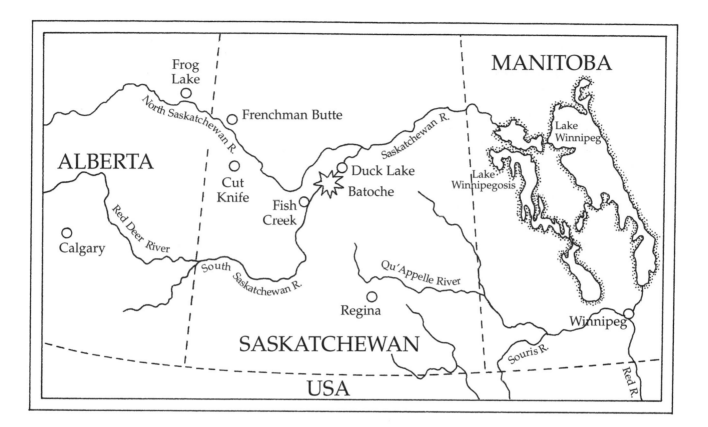

However, some Native chiefs did join the North-West Rebellion. In the south, Poundmaker of the Cree joined the Métis and allowed his braves to loot and burn the settlement of Battleford.

Big Bear
In the north, a Cree chief named Big Bear resisted Indian agent Thomas Quinn's efforts to force the band to settle on a reservation.

Against the wishes of Big Bear, his war chief, Wandering Spirit, attacked Frog Lake on April 2, 1885. Nine white settlers (including Quinn) were massacred and the community was burnt to the ground. Although the aging Big Bear rushed forward to prevent the slaughter, he could not stop the flow of blood. Rebellion came despite Big Bear's efforts.

One of the white prisoners who survived the ordeal at Frog Lake described a scene that occurred three or four days later. Big Bear spoke to 60 seated warriors, including Wandering Spirit. Big Bear ended his speech in loud, angry tones, like the roar of a lion:

"I was a chief. Long ago we fought the Blackfoot, not a man among you could do what I did. All the South Nations — the Bloods, Piegans, Blackfoot,

Crows, Sioux — knew Big Bear, that he was head chief of all the Crees. At that time, if I said anything you listened to me — you obeyed me. But now I say one thing and you do another!"

In a dramatic conclusion, Big Bear swept his arm in front of the faces of Wandering Spirit and the others who sat with lowered eyes, and pointed in the direction of the smouldering ruins of the fort at Frog Lake.

He retained his pose for a moment, his features quivering with emotion, then folded his blanket around himself and strode away.

When the rebellious Wandering Spirit tried to anger the Cree against their prisoners, Big Bear prevented him by speaking in defence of the whites and asking his people to show pity to their captives.

Next, the defiant young Cree braves besieged Fort Pitt. Big Bear used his influence again to arrange for the evacuation of the inhabitants without the loss of their lives. Fort Pitt was burnt by the Cree, but no one was killed.

When the North West Mounted Police arrived with a large force of troops and attacked the Cree at Frenchman Butte, Big Bear's warriors won the battle. But the wise, old chief knew that the struggle was useless. He surrendered, was tried for treason, and found guilty. After serving two years in Stoney Mountain Penitentiary, Big Bear was released but died almost immediately afterward in the winter of 1888.

Martyr or Madman?

Louis Riel deliberately surrendered, instead of escaping to the USA as Gabriel Dumont did. He hoped that in a courtroom he could embarrass the Canadian government into releasing him and recognizing the land rights of the Métis.

Contrary to his lawyer's advice, Riel refused to plead insanity when he was tried for treason in Regina. On August 1, 1885, after only one hour of deliberation, the all-English jury found him guilty and he was sentenced to hang.

Unlocked Prison

After Louis Riel was convicted of treason, Sir John A. Macdonald was swamped with petitions begging him not to execute the rebel. French-speaking Canada was sympathetic to Louis Riel. It was a political dilemma for Macdonald.

Descendants of the North West Mounted Police officers who guarded Riel while he awaited his execution claim that, according to unofficial policy, Louis Riel's cell door was kept unlocked and that a horse with full provisions was saddled and waiting nearby, an open invitation for him to escape to the USA. But Louis stayed and was hanged in 1885.

From Laughter to Regret

At his trial for treason, Big Bear spoke through an interpreter, not for himself but for his people.

"Now I am in chains and will be sent to prison and I have no doubt the handsome faces I admire about me will be competent to govern the land." (laughter from the audience)

"At present I am dead to my people. Many of my band are hiding in the woods, paralysed with terror. Cannot this court send them a pardon? My own children — perhaps they are starving and outcast, too, afraid to appear in the big light of day. If the government does not come to help them before the winter sets in, my band will surely perish . . . I am old and ugly but I have tried to do good. Pity the children of my tribe! Pity the old and helpless of my people! I speak with a single tongue . . . send out and pardon and give them help!"

At the conclusion of his words, the entire court remained in solemn silence.

Design Rebel Trading Cards

Canadian rebels deserve to have their own set of trading cards. Create your own version of Canadian Rebel Trading Cards.

What You Need:
a head-and-shoulder picture or photograph of each Canadian rebel. (You may trace or photocopy them from this or other books, or download them from an internet site, but make sure to credit your source. If you have artistic skills, create your own image of each person.) These must be reduced to a common size to glue onto your cards.
a piece of cardboard for each card (dimensions ie: 6 cm by 9 cm)
glue
a paintbrush or coloured pencils or crayons

What to Do:
1. Design the front of the card.
a) Glue the picture of the rebel on the front of the card. (Decide first on the exact size of the picture. Draw or paint a border around it.)
b) Above or below the picture, type or print the name of the person. (You may wish to type or print the name of the person on a blank piece of paper first and then glue it into place on the card.)

What to Do (continued):

   Note: If you are creating more than one trading card, or if you are play-
   ing this activity with friends or classmates, be certain that you use the
   same size for the pictures and lettering for each card in the series.

2. Design the back of the card.
a) Type or print a brief description of the person. What was the main
    activity that made him or her a rebel?
    For example:
    He was the leader of the Patriote forces in Lower Canada in 1837.
    (Louis-Joseph Papineau)
    He was the only Canadian federal politician to be assassinated.
    (Thomas D'Arcy McGee)
b) You may wish to add another brief description or a nickname.
    For example:
    He is known as "The Father of Manitoba." (Louis Riel)
    He changed his name from Bill Smith to Amor de Cosmos, which means
    "Lover of the Universe."
    (You may wish to type or print the information on a blank piece of paper
    first and then glue it onto the back of the card.)

3. Use your paintbrush, coloured pencils, or crayons to colour the picture
    of the rebel and/or to make colour borders or designs. (You may want
    each card in your series to be a different colour or you may want to have
    the same colours for the whole series.)

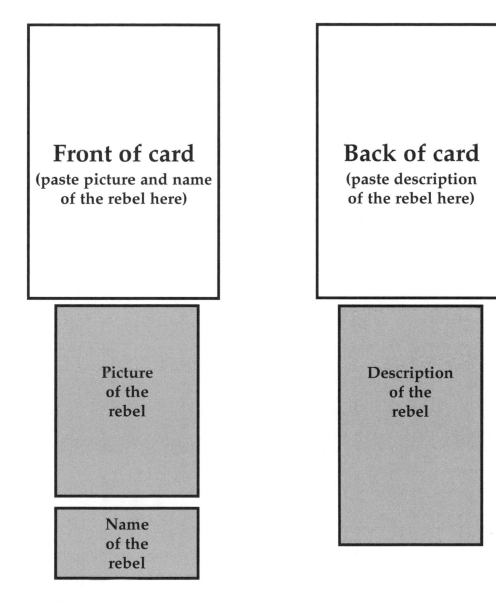

Front of card
(paste picture and name
of the rebel here)

Back of card
(paste description
of the rebel here)

Picture
of the
rebel

Description
of the
rebel

Name
of the
rebel

James Barry, Norman Bethune, and Others

Not all rebels use weapons or words to promote their causes. Some defy social attitudes and conventions with their lifestyles. The way they live their lives becomes a rebellious statement and an example to others.

In 1857, Dr. James Barry was appointed inspector general of hospitals for both Upper and Lower Canada. It was the highest medical appointment in the country. Dr. Barry had authority over hospitals in Montreal, Kingston, Quebec, and Toronto.

After graduating from Edinburgh University in Britain in 1812, James Barry served as a soldier and doctor throughout the world. In Cape Town, Africa, the young doctor performed one of the first cesarean operations in which both mother and child survived. Also in Africa, the concerned physician objected to the poor living conditions of individuals who were kept in the leper colony, the jail, and the lunatic asylum. Reformers were not popular. The critical statements made enemies, who attacked the doctor's personal characteristics with insults.

Dr. Barry was an odd person who strutted rather than walked and had a feminine appearance. The talented surgeon was only 150 centimetres tall, thin and fragile, with small, delicate hands, large eyes, and silky-smooth skin. These physical characteristics caused people to gossip. The fact that the unusual little red-haired doctor refused to drink with the other officers or exchange dirty jokes or stories, only added to their curiosity.

However, no one dared to insult James Barry overtly. The doctor had a quick temper and had already fought one duel over a personal insult. On one occasion, Barry was arrested and sent home under guard because of aggressive behaviour. Despite Barry's unusual personality, everyone respected the surgeon's skill and knowledge of medicine.

Dr. Barry's arrival in Canada as inspector general of hospitals immediately attracted attention and created enemies. James' love of cocked hats with plumes and uniforms decorated with epaulettes created an almost ludicrous appearance. The little doctor paraded around the country, clumsily dragging a sword. Wrapped in musk-ox furs, James rode through the streets of Montreal in a bright red sleigh that was decorated with silver bells. The eccentric physician was always accompanied by a uniformed footman, a coachman, a large black manservant, and a small white dog.

James Barry was a vegetarian, insisting on eating mainly fruit, vegetables, and milk. Despite this personal diet, the doctor, questioning the unhealthy food available for the Canadian troops, demanded that they be fed mutton with salt as well as oven-cooked roasts rather than "the eternal boiled beef and soup."

Striving to improve the living conditions of the soldiers, Dr. Barry declared that sewage disposal and drainage in the barracks were inadequate and unhealthy and that something had to be done. At that time, the married troops slept with their wives in the same barracks as the other soldiers. James insisted the former be given private married quarters. In Canada, as elsewhere, Barry was considered an odd little rebel, although more than competent at the job.

The doctor became ill with bronchitis and influenza and was forced to retire. Six years later, in 1865, James Barry died during a diarrhea epidemic. Major McKinnon, the staff surgeon who signed the death certificate, had never liked Dr. Barry, and so he didn't even examine the corpse.

It was a charwoman, Mrs. Bishop, who discovered the secret of Dr. Barry as she was laying out the body in preparation for burial. Dr. James Barry was a woman! According to Mrs. Bishop, the doctor's body showed clear signs that she had once had a baby.

In those times, it was not possible for a woman to go to university to become a doctor. For 40 years Miranda Stuart had disguised herself as a man named James Barry to enable her to become a medical surgeon. At first, the embarrassed authorities denied the charwoman's story. The body was hurriedly buried.

But the rumours and gossip spread to the newspapers. It was only then that two of Dr. Barry's former associates came forward to support the charwoman's story. In Trinidad, when Dr. Barry had been close to death with yellow fever, the assistant surgeon and another witness had examined her and discovered the secret. She had regained consciousness at that moment and had sworn both of them to secrecy.

Canada's first woman doctor was the world's first woman doctor.

Norman Bethune

Another Canadian doctor with a reputation as a social rebel was Norman Bethune. No one could have predicted that a boy from the small Ontario town of Gravenhurst would become a revolutionary hero to millions in far-away China. He led a highly active life full of violence and danger. In the end, his vision of truth led to his own destruction.

When World War I broke out, Norman was still a student, but he patriotically left medical school and enlisted in the army as a stretcher-bearer. When he went to the rescue of another Canadian soldier during an artillery barrage in Europe, a piece of shrapnel ripped through his leg. He spent the next six months in a hospital.

Back in Toronto, he completed his medical studies and enlisted again, this time as a doctor aboard a warship in the Atlantic.

Deadly Disease

After the war, Bethune chose to help poor people in the slums who could not afford medical treatment. Unexpectedly, he discovered that he was very ill. An X ray indicated that he had pulmonary tuberculosis. There was no cure. He was admitted to the Trudeau Sanatorium in New York State to wait for his certain death.

He decided to spend his last days enjoying life to the fullest. He rebelled against the rules laid down by his doctors. He smoked and drank into the early mornings with the other patients. At that time, it was illegal to drink alcohol, so Bethune was breaking the laws of society as well.

As the deadly disease spread through his body, Bethune read of a new theory in a medical book. It claimed that if the infected lung was deliberately punctured and collapsed, it might prevent the tubercular growth from spreading through his body. His choice was either to live for a few years waiting for certain death or to offer himself as a guinea pig for the untried theory. He gambled and won.

Two months after the operation, he left the sanatorium a cured man. He returned to Montreal to specialize in helping other patients who, like himself, were merely waiting for death. His operating skills as a surgeon became legendary. He wrote medical papers on the subject and invented many new surgical instruments. He became a world-famous thoracic surgeon. He commented on his new outlook on life: "It is only the dull and unimaginative who can lie abed in a sanatorium for a year and fail to rise a better and finer person."

Socialized Medicine

It was the rebel Norman Bethune who fought to introduce socialized medicine to Canada in the 1930s. At that time, the poor were dying because they could not afford medical treatment. His views were considered radical and communistic. At the Verdun YMCA in Montreal, he offered free medical help to the poor.

Spain

When civil war and revolution broke out in Spain in 1936, Bethune travelled overseas to join the Loyalists against Franco's army. Franco's force was aided by other dictators such as Mussolini of Italy and Hitler of Germany, and innocent civilians were being mercilessly slaughtered.

In Spain, Bethune's imagination revolutionized battlefield medicine. With war all around him, he set up a mobile Canadian Blood Transfusion Service. He took blood directly to the wounded on the battlefield. He saved many lives that would have been lost if they had had to wait to be transported back to the hospital. However, Bethune was fighting on the losing side. Dictator Franco and his army were victorious.

China

In 1938, Bethune decided to take his medical talents to Northern China and join the communist rebel army led by Mae Tse-Tung. Mae welcomed Bethune and made him the medical chief of the Red Army. Medical knowledge and facilities were primitive, and Bethune worked without proper equipment, medicine, or finances.

Bethune trained thousands and constantly improvised. For example, he designed a compact field hospital (capable of performing 100 operations and providing 500 dressings) which could be transported through narrow

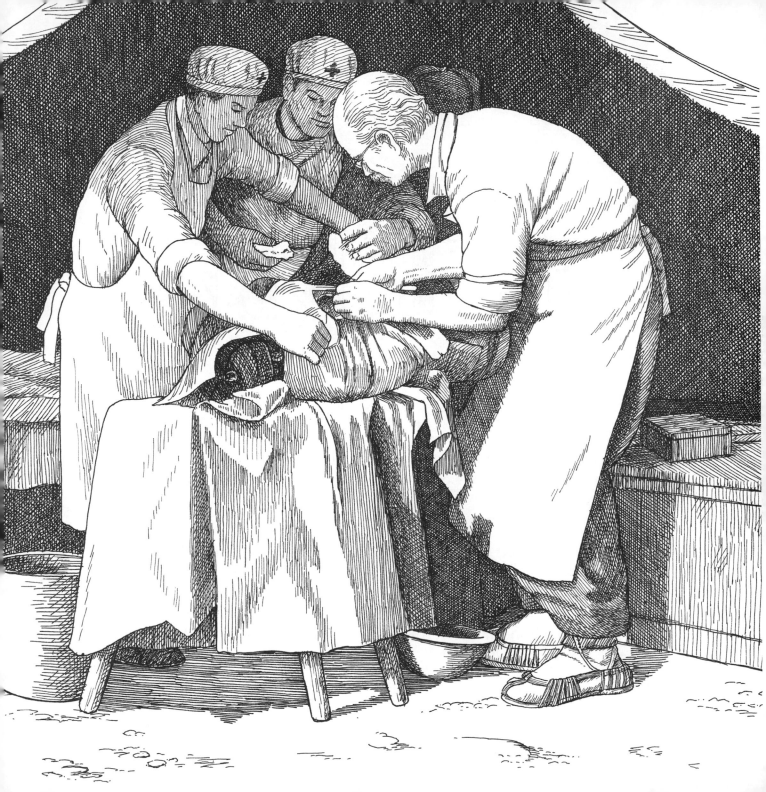

mountain passes on the backs of only two mules. Despite the hardships, he wrote:

> There is no morphine for their pain and when I hurt them, as sometimes I must, they weep the hopeless, overwhelming tears of little children. I have operated all day — 10 cases, 5 of them very serious. I am tired, but I don't think I have been so happy for a long time.

Bethune worked himself to death in his attempts to help the wounded Chinese rebels. A small cut from his own scalpel during an operation caused an infection that spread through his weary body. On November 13, 1939, Dr. Norman Bethune died. And now every November 13, a half a billion Chinese honour the heroic rebel doctor whom they called "Pai Chu En" — "The White One Sent."

Newfoundland Reformer

William Carson, a Scottish doctor, arrived at St. John's in 1808. Alarmed by the poor living conditions in the colony, he demanded social reforms and responsible government. Opponents spread lies about him in the newspapers and in the streets but, by 1832, the outspoken doctor succeeded in establishing Newfoundland's first elected House of Assembly.

Florence Nightingale

The famous nurse Florence Nightingale was serving in the Crimean War when she encountered Dr. James Barry. She did not know that the doctor was a woman. She later complained about the public reprimand that she had received from Barry, as she stood in the hot sun while the doctor sat on a horse.

> "He kept me standing in the midst of quite a crowd of soldiers, commissariat servants, camp followers etc., every one of whom behaved like a gentleman during the scolding I received, while he behaved like a brute. I should say he was the most hardened creature I ever met."

Rebel Women Doctors

When Emily Stowe could not attend medical school in Canada because she was a woman, she travelled to the USA, where some schools were admitting female students. She graduated in 1867 (ten years after Dr. James Barry was chief medical officer in Canada). Emily returned to Canada and opened the first medical practice to be run by a woman, but the Ontario College of Surgeons did not recognize her as a doctor because she had not received her license in Canada. In 1875, another woman, Ginny Trout, also become a doctor in the USA. She then wrote the Canadian exam to become Canada's first recognized female doctor. In 1880, Emily also obtained a license in Canada. Augusta Stowe, Emily's daughter, became the first woman to graduate from a Canadian medical college in January 1883.

Rebel Women Politicians

Nellie McClung was a teacher by the age of 15. She later became a mother of five, an author, and a powerful public speaker before she decided to become a rebel politician. In Canada in the 1800s, a woman was not considered a person in the eyes of the law. She had no legal rights. When she married, all her belongings, her children, and any wages she earned became the property of her husband. It was also legal for a man to beat his wife and children. Nellie fought for women's rights, and on January 27, 1916, succeeded in forcing the politicians in Manitoba to allow women the right to vote and run for political office. A few months later, women won the same rights in Saskatchewan and Alberta. In 1921, Nellie was elected as a member of the Alberta legislature.

In 1917, women who were allowed to vote provincially were permitted to vote federally as well. Agnes Campbell McPhail, from Owen Sound, Ontario, became the first woman to be elected to Canada's parliament in 1921. The last province in Canada to allow women to vote and hold office was Quebec, on April 25, 1940.

Canadian Rebel Crossword Puzzle

ACROSS:

2. His name means "Lover of the Universe."
8. In 1837, this province was known as Lower Canada.
9. The charwoman who discovered the secret of James Barry.
10. Canada and the world's first woman doctor.
11. The tavern that was the headquarters of the rebels in Upper Canada.
13. The country where a rebel doctor worked and died.
15. The term used to describe any Rebel who fought for responsible government.
16. A fort burned by Cree rebels.
17. The rebel leader in Lower Canada.
20. His Chinese name means "The White One Sent."
21. The original name of "Lover of the Universe."
23. The first person killed during the rebellion in Upper Canada.
24. A Loyalist who was executed by Louis Riel.
25. The Métis rebels were defeated at this place.
26. The Fenian Rebel executed for the assassination of Thomas D'Arcy McGee.

DOWN:

1. The famous Canadian police force that fought the Métis rebels.
3. The rebel leader in Upper Canada.
4. The Rebel who was known as "The Father of Manitoba."
5. A rebel Patriote who died at St-Eustache.
6. The province where the North-West Rebellion occurred in 1885.
7. A British officer killed by Patriote rebels in Lower Canada.
8. An Indian agent killed by Cree rebels.
12. The Rebel Louis Riel was tried for treason in this town.
14. A Cree chief found guilty of treason.
18. A disguise used by Rebel Thomas D'Arcy McGee to escape capture.
19. A Métis Rebel known as the "Prince of the Plains."
22. A Canadian doctor aided the Loyalists in this European country.

Canadian Rebel Crossword Puzzle Answers

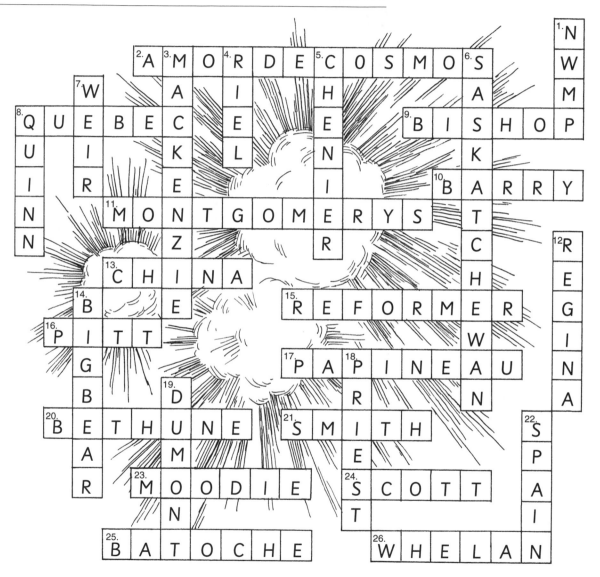

Across and Down answers:

2. AMORDECOSMOS
1. NWMP
5. COSMO
6. SASKATCHEWAN
8. QUEBEC
9. BISHOP
10. BARRY
11. MONTGOMERYS
12. REGINA
13. CHINA
15. REFORMER
16. PITT
17. PAPINEAU
20. BETHUNE
21. SMITH
22. SPAIN
23. MOODIE
24. SCOTT
25. BATOCHE
26. WHELAN

7. WRIR / WAIELKEE
14. BGBAR
19. DUMMN

The Rebels Index